921
SNI

C.1

Blue, Rose.

Wesley Snipes.

34880030013812

$22.95

DATE		

BAKER & TAYLOR

WESLEY SNIPES

WESLEY SNIPES

Rose Blue and Corinne Naden

CHELSEA HOUSE PUBLISHERS
Philadelphia

Chelsea House Publishers

Editor in Chief	Sally Cheney
Production Manager	Pamela Loos
Picture Editor	Judy L. Hasday
Art Director	Sara Davis
Senior Production Editor	J. Christopher Higgins

© 2002 by Chelsea House Publishers, a subsidiary of Haights Cross
Communications. All rights reserved. Printed and bound in the
United States of America.

The Chelsea House World Wide Web address is
http://www.chelseahouse.com

First Printing

1 3 5 7 9 8 6 4 2

Blue, Rose.
    Wesley Snipes / Rose Blue and Corinne Naden.
        p. cm.—(Black Americans of achievement)
    Filmography: p.
    Includes bibliographical references and index.
    Summary: A biography of the black American actor whose films
include "White Men Can't Jump," "Demolition Man," and "Wait-
ing to Exhale."
    ISBN 0-7910-5800-X (HC : alk. paper)—ISBN 0-7910-5801-8
(PB : alk. paper)
    1. Snipes, Wesley—Juvenile literature. 2. Motion picture actors
and actresses—United States—Biography—Juvenile literature. 3.
African American motion picture actors and actresses—United
States—Biography—Juvenile literature. [1. Snipes, Wesley. 2.
Actors and actresses. 3. African Americans—Biography.] I. Naden,
Corinne J. II. Title. III. Series.

PN2287.S618 B59 2001
791.43'028'092—dc21
[B]   2001042097

*Frontispiece: Wesley Snipes
has crafted a unique career
from the diverse roles he has
played on screen. From
action star to ladies' man,
Snipes has fashioned himself
into one of today's most rec-
ognizable celebrities.*

CONTENTS

BLACK AMERICANS OF ACHIEVEMENT

HENRY AARON
baseball great

KAREEM ABDUL-JABBAR
basketball great

MUHAMMAD ALI
heavyweight champion

RICHARD ALLEN
religious leader and social activist

MAYA ANGELOU
author

LOUIS ARMSTRONG
musician

ARTHUR ASHE
tennis great

JOSEPHINE BAKER
entertainer

JAMES BALDWIN
author

TYRA BANKS
model

BENJAMIN BANNEKER
scientist and mathematician

COUNT BASIE
bandleader and composer

ANGELA BASSETT
actress

ROMARE BEARDEN
artist

HALLE BERRY
actress

MARY MCLEOD BETHUNE
educator

GEORGE WASHINGTON
CARVER
botanist

JOHNNIE COCHRAN
lawyer

BILL COSBY
entertainer

MILES DAVIS
musician

FREDERICK DOUGLASS
abolitionist editor

CHARLES DREW
physician

W. E. B. DU BOIS
scholar and activist

PAUL LAURENCE DUNBAR
poet

DUKE ELLINGTON
bandleader and composer

RALPH ELLISON
author

JULIUS ERVING
basketball great

LOUIS FARRAKHAN
political activist

ELLA FITZGERALD
singer

ARETHA FRANKLIN
entertainer

MORGAN FREEMAN
actor

MARCUS GARVEY
black nationalist leader

JOSH GIBSON
baseball great

WHOOPI GOLDBERG
entertainer

CUBA GOODING JR.
actor

ALEX HALEY
author

PRINCE HALL
social reformer

JIMI HENDRIX
musician

MATTHEW HENSON
explorer

GREGORY HINES
performer

BILLIE HOLIDAY
singer

LENA HORNE
entertainer

WHITNEY HOUSTON
singer and actress

LANGSTON HUGHES
poet

JANET JACKSON
musician

JESSE JACKSON
civil-rights leader and politician

MICHAEL JACKSON
entertainer

SAMUEL L. JACKSON
actor

T. D. JAKES
religious leader

JACK JOHNSON
heavyweight champion

MAGIC JOHNSON
basketball great

SCOTT JOPLIN
composer

BARBARA JORDAN
politician

MICHAEL JORDAN
basketball great

CORETTA SCOTT KING
civil-rights leader

MARTIN LUTHER KING, JR.
civil-rights leader

LEWIS LATIMER
scientist

SPIKE LEE
filmmaker

CARL LEWIS
champion athlete

JOE LOUIS
heavyweight champion

RONALD MCNAIR
astronaut

MALCOLM X
militant black leader

BOB MARLEY
musician

THURGOOD MARSHALL
Supreme Court justice

TERRY MCMILLAN
author

TONI MORRISON
author

ELIJAH MUHAMMAD
religious leader

EDDIE MURPHY
entertainer

JESSE OWENS
champion athlete

SATCHEL PAIGE
baseball great

CHARLIE PARKER
musician

ROSA PARKS
civil-rights leader

COLIN POWELL
military leader

PAUL ROBESON
singer and actor

JACKIE ROBINSON
baseball great

CHRIS ROCK
comedian and actor

DIANA ROSS
entertainer

WILL SMITH
actor

WESLEY SNIPES
actor

CLARENCE THOMAS
Supreme Court justice

SOJOURNER TRUTH
antislavery activist

HARRIET TUBMAN
antislavery activist

NAT TURNER
slave revolt leader

TINA TURNER
entertainer

ALICE WALKER
author

MADAM C. J. WALKER
entrepreneur

BOOKER T. WASHINGTON
educator

DENZEL WASHINGTON
actor

J. C. WATTS
politician

VANESSA WILLIAMS
singer and actress

OPRAH WINFREY
entertainer

TIGER WOODS
golf star

RICHARD WRIGHT
author

ON ACHIEVEMENT

Coretta Scott King

Before you begin this book, I hope you will ask yourself what the word *excellence* means to you. I think it's a question we should all ask, and keep asking as we grow older and change. Because the truest answer to it should never change. When you think of excellence, perhaps you think of success at work; or of becoming wealthy; or meeting the right person, getting married, and having a good family life.

Those goals are worth striving for, but there is a better way to look at excellence. As Martin Luther King Jr. said in one of his last sermons, "I want you to be first in love. I want you to be first in moral excellence. I want you to be first in generosity. If you want to be important, wonderful. If you want to be great, wonderful. But recognize that he who is greatest among you shall be your servant."

My husband knew that the true meaning of achievement is service. When I met him, in 1952, he was already ordained as a Baptist minister and was working toward a doctoral degree at Boston University. I was studying at the New England Conservatory and dreamed of accomplishments in music. We married a year later, and after I graduated the following year we moved to Montgomery, Alabama. We didn't know it then, but our notions of achievement were about to undergo a dramatic change.

You may have read or heard about what happened next. What began with the boycott of a local bus line grew into a national crusade, and by the time he was assassinated in 1968 my husband had fashioned a black movement powerful enough to shatter forever the practice of racial segregation. What you may not have read about is where he learned to resist injustice without compromising his religious beliefs.

He adopted a strategy of nonviolence from a man of a different race, who lived in a different country and even practiced a different religion. The man was Mahatma Gandhi, the great leader of India, who devoted his life to serving humanity in the spirit of love and nonviolence. It was in these principles that Martin discovered his method for social reform. More than anything else, those two principles were the key to his achievements.

These books are about African Americans who served society through the excellence of their achievements. They form part of the rich history of black men and women in America—a history of stunning accomplishments in every field of human endeavor, from literature and art to science, industry, education, diplomacy, athletics, jurisprudence, even polar exploration.

Not all of the people in this history had the same ideals, but I think you will find that all of them had something in common. Like Martin Luther King Jr., they all decided to become "drum majors" and serve humanity. In that principle—whether it was expressed in books, inventions, or song—they found a goal and a guide outside themselves that showed them a way to serve others instead of living only for themselves.

Reading the stories of these courageous men and women not only helps us discover the principles that we will use to guide our own lives; it also teaches us about our black heritage and about America itself. It is crucial for us to know the heroes and heroines of our history and to realize that the price we paid in our struggle for equality in America was dear. But we must also understand that we have gotten as far as we have partly because America's democratic system and ideals made it possible.

We are still struggling with racism and prejudice. But the great men and women in this series are a tribute to the spirit of the country in which they have flourished. And that makes their stories special and worth knowing.

1

THE ORLANDO-BRONX CONNECTION

◦◦◦

ONE OF THE big tourist attractions in Los Angeles is the Hollywood Walk of Fame, where luminaries of the acting world have been immortalized by bronze stars and footprints—or in the case of Lassie the collie, pawprints—that line both sides of a five-acre stretch of Hollywood Boulevard and Vine Street. Although the project was started in 1958, the first prints didn't go down in cement until 1960 (these belonged to Oscar winner Joanne Woodward). In 1978, the Walk was designated as a historic landmark.

Today the Hollywood Chamber of Commerce adds two new bronze stars and four new footprints to the sidewalks each month. On August 21, 1998, it was Walk-of-Fame day for Wesley Snipes, a black American actor not only with his footprints cast in cement but his feet planted firmly on the ground.

The story of how Wesley Snipes got to the Walk of Fame begins clear across the country in Orlando, Florida, a place almost as well known as Hollywood and for the same reason. Both locales are home to great entertainment centers. Disney World is located about sixteen miles southwest of Orlando. But the city can boast other distinctions. It's the center of the state's citrus fruit area. It's the site of the University of Central Florida. And it's the hometown of Wesley Snipes.

Having one's name preserved on the famous Hollywood Walk of Fame is a highlight in almost any celebrity's career. Wesley poses here during the unveiling of his star on the prestigious walk.

Growing up in the projects of the South Bronx was hard, but Wesley was encouraged by his family to find ways to stay out of trouble. His mother encouraged Wesley to spend much of his time at a nearby YMCA instead of becoming involved with life on the streets.

Snipes was born in Orlando in the heat of the Florida summer, on July 31, 1962. His mother was a teaching assistant, his father an aircraft engineer. Within two years of Wesley's birth, his father had left home, and a divorce followed. For years, Wesley had no contact with or memory of his dad.

Soon after her divorce, Marian Snipes decided to leave Orlando, moving her son and a younger daughter named Brigette northward to the Bronx, a borough of New York City, to be closer to members of her family.

Wesley grew up in the area known as the South Bronx in what he calls a "boogie-down" neighborhood. It was a rough, no-nonsense, blue collar, minority kind of place, mainly filled with blacks and Latinos. His family was poor, not middle class, and his mother had to work two jobs to support them.

The South Bronx has never been called an easy place to grow up. Yet the area boasts a good number of people who not only grew up there but went on to fame and fortune. One of the most famous is Colin Powell, who grew up on Kelly Street, a former chairman of the Joint Chiefs of Staff and Secretary of State under President George W. Bush. Like so many Bronx residents today,

BOASTING TIME IN THE BRONX

The Bronx owes its name to Jonas Bronck, a Scandinavian, who bought some five hundred acres of land in 1641. Today, the Bronx covers forty-one square miles and is the only one of New York City's five boroughs to be on the mainland. The other four—Manhattan, Queens, Brooklyn, and Staten Island—are all islands and connected to the Bronx and each other by tunnels and bridges.

The Bronx boasts two outstanding sites that attract visitors from all over. One is Yankee Stadium, built in 1923 and home to the winningest club in baseball, the New York Yankees. Around home, the team is also known as the Bronx Bombers and the stadium as the House That Ruth Built, in honor of Babe Ruth, (1895–1948), who joined the Yankees in 1920. Ruth was not only an excellent left-handed pitcher, with a record of ninety-four wins and forty-six losses, but arguably the game's greatest hitter. His statistics are staggering: a lifetime batting average of .342; a lifetime home run total of 714 (which stood unbroken until Hank Aaron hit 715 in 1974); a record of sixty home runs in one season (which stood until Roger Maris hit sixty-one in 1961). In anyone's list of the greatest baseball figures who ever played the game, Babe Ruth is usually number one.

The other great tourist attraction in the Bronx is the New York Zoological Park, better known as the Bronx Zoo. The zoo opened in 1899 and covers 252 acres. In 1941, the African Plains was completed; in the 1960s, this area was widely expanded, allowing great varieties of animals to roam freely. Today visitors traveling on a monorail can visit a wide array of exhibits.

Powell's parents were immigrants. They came to New York City from Jamaica in the 1920s and found jobs in the garment district. Their idea was that even in a rough neighborhood, children could be taught the right values in life. It certainly worked for General Powell. And it worked for Wesley Snipes, too.

Wesley's early childhood years were shaped not only by the turbulent life in the South Bronx but by the America of the 1960s—an era that was frantic, sometimes scary, often violent.

The violence began early in the decade, on November 22, 1963, when President John F. Kennedy was killed by assassin Lee Harvey Oswald in Dallas, Texas. For the eighth time in the nation's history, a president had died in office, the fourth to be killed by an assassin. The other assassinated presidents were Abraham Lincoln, who was shot by John Wilkes Booth at Ford's Theatre, in Washington, D.C., on April 15, 1865; James Garfield, shot by Charles J. Guiteau in the Washington, D.C., train depot on July 2, 1881, and died in Elberon, N.J., on September 19; and William McKinley, shot on September 6, 1901, in Buffalo, N.Y., by an out-of-work millhand from Detroit named Leon F. Czolgosz. McKinley died on September 14. Then there was John Kennedy, shot while traveling in a motorcade through the streets of Dallas with his wife, Jackie, beside him.

On November 24, the country was barely able to deal with the shock of Kennedy's death while his assassin, Oswald, was killed as Dallas police were transferring him from one prison to another. A nightclub owner named Jack Ruby had calmly walked up to Oswald and shot him, as television cameras recorded the event for a horrified nation.

Americans were also getting edgy in the 1960s about the continuing cold war with Russia and about a war in far-off Vietnam. That war would drag on through many years of political debate, student

protests, and draft resistance until 1975, affecting the lives of most Americans in the process.

Another kind of fight was also going on at home in America. Fed up with endless promises of equality for all Americans, both black and white began to demand civil rights legislation. The Reverend Martin Luther King Jr. emerged as the movement's leader, advocating nonviolent protest, organizing march after march until his own death by an assassin on April 4, 1968, in Memphis, Tennessee. Two months later, the nation had to deal with yet another assassination. Robert F. Kennedy, brother of the late president, was fatally shot while campaigning for the Democratic presidential nomination in California.

Beyond all the violence and protest, however, there were some social and cultural milestones that

The 1960s was a turbulent time of civil change and tragic violence. The entire country was shocked when Lee Harvey Oswald, seen here at center, shot and killed President Kennedy.

left an imprint on the decade—from the Beatles crossing the Atlantic and throwing the entire adolescent population into a tizzy and changing the American music scene, to the gathering of a rock generation at Woodstock, to the historic moment on July 20, 1969, when perhaps one billion people sat mesmerized in front of their television sets as American astronaut Neil A. Armstrong climbed down from his *Eagle* landing craft and scuffed up some dust from the surface of the moon.

Growing up in this fast-moving decade was a challenge, made harder if you were growing up in the South Bronx, in poor neighborhoods where children were often prey to drugs and crime and the lure of easy money. Wesley's mother was not about to let that happen to her children. "She kept a close eye," says Snipes of his mother.

One of his mother's ideas to keep seven-year-old Wesley out of trouble was to enroll him in a martial arts class held at the Harlem YMCA. Martial arts would become a lifelong interest for Snipes and an integral part of his movie career.

Other women were watching out for Wesley, too, among them his aunt, Della Saunders, who took a strong interest in her nephew and played a large part in recognizing his talent and developing his interest in show business.

"Most people in my family are women," says Wesley. "I grew up in a house with three women. My aunt had three daughters. My baby sitter had three daughters. And I was the Girl Scout helper when I was nine or ten. I sold cookies so I could get to go on field trips."

As a young boy, Snipes was small for his age. He was only five feet five inches tall even in high school but would add another six inches by adulthood. Perhaps because of his short height, he developed what he himself admits was a "Napoleon complex." He became a bold showoff, what he calls a "slickster." He

America lost one of its most important figures when Dr. Martin Luther King Jr. was killed by an assassin's bullet in 1968.

Two boys take part in a judo lesson and learn both the technique and discipline of the martial arts. The martial arts were a major influence in Wesley's early life, and many of his future roles as an actor have reflected his martial arts training.

was smart and he knew it and he knew he could get away with it.

Well, almost. There was always his mother and Aunt Della looking on.

"It's a good thing they were," Snipes says today. For among the young boy's "slickster" pastimes was the pool hall, and he became quite good at the game. But pool halls in the neighborhood were often the scene of petty crime and drug dealings. The tough guys hung around there and Wesley wanted to be one of them. His mother had other ideas.

HARLEM YMCA: A LONG AND DISTINGUISHED HISTORY

The Harlem YMCA has been helping young men like Wesley Snipes since 1919 when it opened its doors at the center of Harlem life and business activity. Over the years it has established a vital presence in the community. Besides sponsoring martial arts classes, such as those young Wesley attended, the YMCA has a gym and aerobics studio, gives swimming lessons, and even has guest rooms for out-of-towners or a Harlem relative needing a place to stay while visiting. The focus is still on young people and teens, and more than 200 volunteers give their time yearly to make these programs work.

2

FORTH AND BACK

❧

THE LATE AND great jazz pianist Fats Waller (1904–1943) was once asked what advice he would give to an aspiring musician wanting to know whether he or she has the right stuff and a chance for success. Replied the ever expressive Fats, "Hey, if you gotta ask, you don't got it."

But if you've got it, you usually show it early. And if you're lucky, someone else recognizes it. In Wesley's case, it was Aunt Della. She didn't ask; she just knew. Della figured that the "showoff" aspect of her nephew's personality could be put to good use and she began to enter him in talent shows. Aunt Della became a self-proclaimed stage aunt, talent scout, and agent. She must have been pretty good at it, for when Wesley was twelve, he began his show biz career. He got a small part in the off-Broadway production of *The Me Nobody Knows*. Off Broadway was a long way from Broadway; it wasn't much, but it was a start.

At that time, Snipes was attending PS 131, also known as Albert Einstein Intermediate School. The school is still there on Bolton Avenue in the South Bronx. When Wesley wasn't at basketball practice, Aunt Della tried to keep him busy with auditions. With his interest growing in a show business career, he also joined an after-school drama program.

A talented performer with strong skills in both drama and dance, Wesley demonstrated an interest in becoming an entertainer from an early age.

At school his drama teachers also knew talent when they saw it. In fact, they thought Wesley had so much talent that they figured he might be accepted at New York City's renowned High School of the Performing Arts. But then, Aunt Della could have told them that.

Having talent and getting accepted are two different things altogether. And in the case of this high school, getting accepted is not easy.

In 1936, then mayor of New York City Fiorello H. LaGuardia, affectionately known as the Little Flower, founded the High School of Music and Art. The idea was to give the city's talented public school students a place to learn their craft and get a good education as well. In 1948, a second school—the School of Performing Arts—was created for youngsters who sought a career in dance, music, or acting. In 1961, the two schools became one organization and, in 1984, merged into a single building in New York City's Lincoln Center complex. Formally known as the Fiorello H. LaGuardia High School of Music and Art and Peforming Arts, it is one of four specialized high schools in the city, the other three—Stuyvesant, Bronx Science, and Brooklyn Technical High School—specializing in the sciences.

The School of Performing Arts was the model for the film and TV series *Fame*. The title song, performed by aspiring students, is an apt description of their dreams:

> I'm gonna make it to heaven
> Light up the sky like a flame. . .
> I'm gonna live forever
> Baby, remember my name.

The requirements for admission to LaGuardia High are much the same today as when Snipes

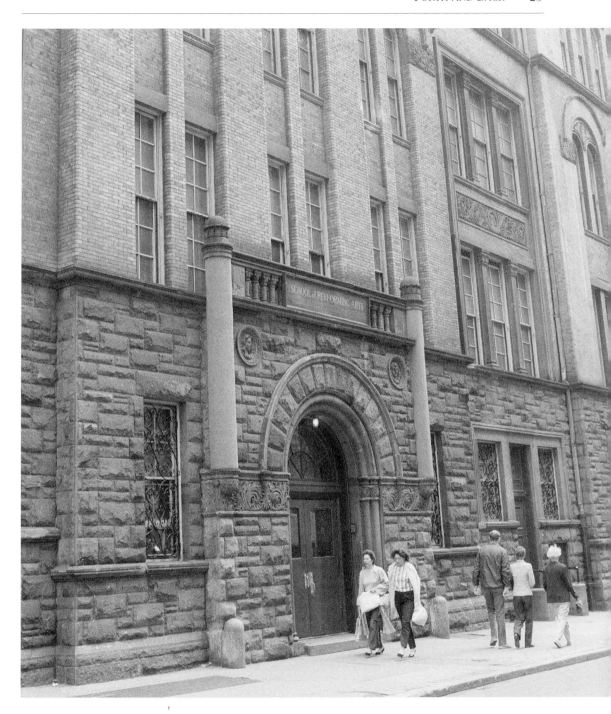

The entrance to the School of Performing Arts in New York City. Being accepted into the highly competitive school was an important moment in young Wesley's life.

A group of students take part in a "play fight" during a drama class. Classes at the School of Performing Arts helped shape Wesley's dramatic skills.

entered. To be eligible, the applicant must be a resident of New York City and in the eighth or ninth grade. Enrollment is 2,500 students, students must pass rigorous entrance auditions, and almost all of the school's graduates go on to higher education.

The entrance examinations, which Snipes, like all other applicants, had to pass before acceptance, are daunting. Aspiring artists take a three-hour test that includes drawing from a live model, drawing a still life from memory, and illustrating an assigned topic, such as a summer day at the ocean. Applicants must also bring to the audition ten to twenty pieces of original artwork.

Aspiring musicians are asked to play at least one selection, to sight-read, and to tap back a rhythmic pattern that is tapped out by an instructor. Singers are asked to sing short melodies that are being played and also to perform one vocal selection.

Aspiring dancers will be evaluated by a panel of as many as seven instructors. Applicants are placed in groups of twenty to twenty-five students and are given a modified ballet class and then a modern dance class. Some students may be asked to perform a solo dance. Each dancer is given a grade from 1 to 100. Those who get less than 80 don't get in.

Aspiring actors will be asked to deliver a monologue in front of a panel of critics. Students are supplied with a suggested list of plays from which to choose a monologue, such as *Biloxi Blues* by Neil Simon for a young man or *A Raisin in the Sun* by Lorraine Hansberry for a young woman. The performers are evaluated for energy, good use of self, ability to communicate the circumstances of the scene to an audience, and overall acting composure.

Once accepted, a student at LaGuardia also has to concentrate on academic studies. Four years of English and social studies are required, plus math, foreign languages, sciences, and all the other requirements for a regular high school. In addition, there are sports and physical education classes.

One way of telling the worth of a school is by the success of its students. LaGuardia boasts thousands of successful alumni in the world of entertainment and in other fields, some who graduated, some who spent only a year or two. The roster includes such actors as Al Pacino, Dom DeLuise, Suzanne Pleschette, and Richard Benjamin, singers Liza Minelli and Eartha Kitt, plus journalists such as Max Frankel, editor of the *New York Times*. In addition, there are lawyers, architects, doctors, scientists, and businesspeople all over the country who got a start at LaGuardia.

Although Wesley's future led to acting, as a young man he hoped to become a dancer, like the renowned Alvin Ailey.

Members of the Alvin Ailey American Dance Company take part in a performance. Wesley still wonders if he could have had a career as a dancer in a company like Ailey's.

To young Wesley Snipes, getting accepted at the High School of Performing Arts was more than a dream come true. At first, he thought of becoming a dancer, but he also took classes in acting. "It was a great experience totally. I loved every aspect of it. I got a lot of positive response," Snipes recalls. But he is still wistful about a might-have-been dancing career. "I still have a latent passion for that. When I see Alvin Ailey or Chuck Davis, I'm sitting there saying 'I could have been there.'"

Although Snipes loved his acting and dancing classes and generally got along well in school, he encountered trouble with after-school activities. The various things that occupied his fellow classmates—the school newspaper, athletic teams, student government, the art club—held no interest for Wesley, who was still drawn to the local pool hall.

As he explained to his mother, he was very good at playing pool and it provided him with an easy cash flow. Snipes was pleased with himself, but his mother was faced with exactly what she'd been fearing for years: companions and activities that were bound to get him into trouble and ruin any chance of a successful career. She decided to take action. If she couldn't take the South Bronx out of the boy, she'd just take the boy out of the South Bronx, back to Orlando.

When she confronted her teenaged son in 1977 with the news, he was stunned. Take him out of this amazing school when he had just two years to go, take him away from the city that was every performer's dream? No way!

"No way" turned into his mother's way. No amount of pleading and carrying on would change her mind. She had seen the handwriting—or perhaps the graffiti—on too many South Bronx walls. This was not the right atmosphere for Wesley at this time. Besides, she had family still living in Orlando. They would be a good influence on the young man. In addition, back in Orlando she could afford a three-bedroom house rather than the cramped apartment they now occupied.

Wesley Snipes could gripe all he wanted, but Marian had made her decision. The family headed back down to Orlando.

3
DRAMA TIME

HOW WESLEY SNIPES could relate to the words in Frank Sinatra's megahit, *New York, New York*, especially the line, "I wanna be a part of it, New York, New York."

Here he was, dragged out of the mecca of the entertainment world, the place where every budding star wants to be, the city "that never sleeps," the frenzy of life in the fast lane to . . . nowhere. Sure he had sunshine and palm trees. He had family members all around him too, but, well, Orlando was just so slow.

At first, he fought it. "If I could have walked back to New York, I would have," he recalls. It was so difficult to adjust to a slower-paced way of life. "They're just moseying along, like lemonade on the porch on a Sunday afternoon. . . ." Years later, Snipes would admit that the move was the best thing that could have happened to him at that time, that as expected many of his old buddies eventually found themselves in deep trouble back in the South Bronx. But for the present, anyway, all he could say was "Take me back to New York."

What saved Snipes from complete desolation was another high school—Jones High, a mainly black public school in Orlando. Maybe it wasn't the High School for the Performing Arts, but it had a superior drama department.

Wesley Snipes's transition from New York to Orlando was a difficult one, but he found some solace in the fact that his new school had an excellent drama department and he could continue to pursue his acting dream.

In short order, Snipes became the star of the school's drama department. It didn't hurt that he had attended an elite high school in New York, nor was he shy about telling everybody! But he was warmly welcomed and soon appeared in the school's production of *Damn Yankees*. He won an award for playing Puck in *A Midsummer Night's Dream*, adapting Shakespeare's character to a one-man show. In addition, he played the role of Felix Ungar in *The Odd Couple*, a comedy about two divorced men living together made famous on film by Jack Lemmon as the fussy Felix and Walter Matthau as the sloppy Oscar. Instead of shooting pool for spending money, Snipes joined a city drama troupe called Struttin' Street Stuff and made money by putting on puppet shows in schools and parks. This pleased his mother to no end.

Karen Rugerio was Wesley's drama teacher at Jones High. Now a teacher at Dr. Phillips High in Orlando, Rugerio remains close to him today and talked about her student and the Jones drama program in an interview for this book.

"We did cutting edge theater. When you have kids that talented, it's important to seek quality stuff for them to do," she says. "Wesley was always very focused. He was a little skinny, wiry kid. A terrific agile, deep-voiced actor. In *Raisin in the Sun*, he played an eight-year-old. He also played in our black version of *The Odd Couple*. At Jones High, we came out with a black version of that comedy before Broadway did!"

Rugerio remembers that Snipes never had problems with actors of any color playing any role. His acting and dancing skills singled him out clearly as a "dynamic actor." "I recall his terrific acrobatics when he played Puck in *A Midsummer Night's Dream*," she says. "He also did a duet from *West Side Story* and won an award in the Florida competition."

Wesley poses with members of his family, including his mother, Marian, and his aunt, Della, during his induction into Hollywood's Walk of Fame. Also attending the ceremony was Karen Rugerio, a high school drama teacher who nurtured Wesley's love of performing and with whom he remains close.

According to Rugerio, the actor's personal traits have remained admirable, especially his loyalty to those who have been close to him and have helped him. For instance, when his movie *Blade* opened in Hollywood in 1998 and he was inducted into the Hollywood Walk of Fame, among the people who were his guests was Karen Rugerio. "He paid for everything," she recalls with a smile, "and took care of us first class." Wesley has also remained close with his two best friends from high school, Victor McGouley and Eddie Powell Cosby. McGouley now works in the office of Snipes's business manager in Los Angeles, and the actor still keeps in touch with Cosby, who remained in Orlando.

Wesley Snipes graduated from Jones High in 1980 and never forgot his time well spent there. Today, when he can, he returns to Orlando and attends seminars at Jones, talks to the students, conducts workshops, and tries to "give back" what he was given. Says Rugerio, "He tries to teach kids what he has learned." He remembers his school days in New York as well. Snipes set up a foundation without publicizing his name that does charity work involving youngsters in poor neighborhoods.

Despite such attachments in Orlando, Wesley had not forgotten the magic of Broadway either. So, when it was time for college, naturally he headed north to New York. He was accepted into the intensely competitive theater arts program at the State University of New York (SUNY) at Purchase, about an hour's drive north of New York City. The competition for entrance to the program was fierce, yet Snipes not only was accepted but received a scholarship, named for Victor Borge, the Danish-born pianist/comedian.

As Snipes explains it, the objective at Purchase is "to prepare you to be a multifaceted, well-trained actor for the classical American stage." And it takes its training seriously. Just ask Lawrence Kornfeld,

Wesley attended SUNY Purchase, participating in the university's highly competitive theater arts program. About 80 percent of the program's graduates go on to find work as actors.

Wesley strolls to the set during the filming of one of his pictures. The intensive training he received during his college years at SUNY Purchase have served him well in the demanding world of filmmaking.

professor of theater arts at SUNY and fomer dean. In an interview for this book, Kornfeld explains the reasoning behind SUNY's approach. "If you are serious about a stage career," he says, "you need to try for conservatory-style training. A conservatory is an advanced school of specialized training in an area of the arts that emphasizes technical instruction and practical performance. The program at SUNY is now known as the Conservatory of Theatre Arts and Film, and its major focus is to train students for professional careers. "The conservatory is for serious students," says Kornfeld. "The training here is strong. Our students spend three times as much time acting and have three times as much faculty supervision as other schools. It's a respected school—similar to Juilliard in respect—and very difficult to get into." Juilliard is the prestigious conservatory of music in New York City.

To get into the program at Purchase, Snipes had to once again audition. The demands make it easy to believe that SUNY takes its training very seriously indeed. For admittance to the freshman class, prospective students must audition either at the Purchase campus itself or at designated locations from New York to Chicago to Los Angeles. The four-minute audition consists of two monologues delivered by the student—one using classical material, the other contemporary.

Once admitted, the student becomes part of a small select class that operates as a working theater company. Besides such basic courses as history of the theater, movement for actors, dramatic literature, and voice, students must also take courses in make-up, gymnastics, circus arts, stage combat, fencing, and mask work, among others. The intense and comprehensive training clearly pays off. About 80 percent of SUNY's graduates find employment as actors.

Professor Kornfeld taught Snipes at Purchase and remembers him well. "Wesley was a very serious student," he says, "and extremely intent about acting.

Snipes is seen here in 1998 upon receiving his honorary doctoral degree from SUNY Purchase.

He was outspoken about racism and proud to be black, but he felt that acting should know no race." Kornfeld directed Snipes in Bertolt Brecht's *The Good Woman of Setzuan*, a musical parable set in China. Snipes played the role of the landlord and did it in whiteface. "He was brilliant," says his teacher. "But he could have been a great dancer, too. He has wonderful control of his body." Kornfeld spoke of Snipes as accomplished, superb, dynamic, with a personality "as dynamic offscreen as he is on." Another acting teacher at SUNY, David Garfield, spoke of Snipes as "obviously gifted. He was extremely funny. He could do straight drama, he could sing, and he would stop shows with the dance numbers he had choreographed."

Obviously, Wesley's years at SUNY had a great impact on his life and career. He still goes back and spends time with the new students and is very active in causes with young people. In 1998, he became "Doctor Snipes" when his alma mater awarded him an honorary doctorate degree in humanities and fine arts.

It's not uncommon for students in the SUNY drama program to audition for roles in an upcoming legitimate theater production or a motion picture. Snipes heard that famous folk and calypso singer Harry Belafonte was coproducing a movie about urban ghetto kids who upgrade themselves by developing breakdancing routines. It seemed a perfect vehicle for an aspiring young dancer, so Snipes auditioned. Unfortunately, he didn't make the cast. The movie came out in 1984 to mediocre reviews.

Snipes worked and studied hard through his four years in college. But his career was not the only thing on his mind. As a young man in search of his roots, he could not escape the fact that at Purchase he was just one of four black students in the theater arts program. As he later described it, he felt "like mold on white bread." In his quest for a new awareness, Snipes turned to the religion of Islam.

4

FOOD FOR THE SOUL

WHILE HE WAS a student at SUNY, Wesley Snipes saw a documentary about the charismatic Black Muslim leader Malcolm X. "It changed my whole life," he said, "everything. After I saw the film, I went straight to the library, took out his autobiography, and for two days, I just read. It saved me." The book that so entranced Snipes, *The Autobiography of Malcolm X*, was cowritten with well-known black writer Alex Haley. Haley is also the author of *Roots*, the best-selling novel on which the miniseries of the same name is based. *The Autobiography of Malcolm X* is considered a classic of black American autobiography.

Snipes felt renewed after learning about Malcolm X. He said, "A brother of mine used to say that when you're drowning, 'grab on to a log to keep afloat. But don't hold on to the log when the boat comes by. Get on the boat and bring yourself back home!' Islam for me was the log to make me more conscious of what African people have accomplished, of my self-worth, and it gave me some self-dignity."

SUNY teacher David Garfield was there to observe the new direction that Snipes took. "He exhibited a strong black consciousness even then." Because of that strong sense and because of the influence of Malcolm X, Wesley Snipes converted to the Islamic faith while in college.

As an African American, Wesley has maintained a strong sense of cultural identity. Part of the credit for this, he says, belongs to Malcolm X, whose autobiography Wesley discovered while in college.

Malcolm X was a powerful figure whose words and actions inspired Wesley to learn more about both black culture and the teachings of Islam.

The religion that so impressed Wesley Snipes—and its one billion followers—is Islam, one of the world's major faiths. The word *islam* means "surrender" or "submit" in Arabic. Followers of Islam, known as Muslims, are thus expected to surrender themselves to the will of God or *Allah* in Arabic. The will of God is found in the Koran, Islam's sacred writings, which were revealed to the prophet Muhammad back in the seventh century A.D.

Muhammad was born about A.D. 570 in Mecca, in what is today Saudi Arabia. The famous shrine in the center of Mecca, said to have been built by the prophet Abraham for the worship of one god, was in fact filled with many idols of wood, stone, or clay. There was no single king nor any one religion in the region of Arabia, a poor land of mostly desert and scrub. Many Arabs were nomads tending their sheep or selling goods from town to town, traveling by camel in groups called caravans.

Orphaned at an early age, Muhammad went on caravan journeys with his uncle. On one such journey he met and married a wealthy widow and trader, Khadijah, who was fifteen years his senior. Their marriage lasted twenty-five years and they had six

MALCOLM X: BLACK MUSLIM LEADER

Malcolm X was born Malcolm Little in Omaha, Nebraska, in 1925. His early years growing up in Michigan were marred by tragedy: his house was burned by members of the racist Ku Klux Klan, his father was later murdered, and his mother was placed in a mental institution. After a troubled youth, he spent six years in prison for burglary. While there he was converted to an Islamic sect known as the Black Muslims (Nation of Islam), a group that preached the evil of the white race.

After his release from prison, Malcolm joined Black Muslim leader Elijah Muhammad in Chicago and added the X to his name, following the custom observed by Black Muslims who consider their family names to have come from white slaveowners.

Malcolm X left Chicago to become minister of Mosque Number Seven in New York's Harlem district. He was a brilliant speaker and soon won a large following. But because he advocated violence for self-protection, many civil rights leaders of the time thought him to be a fanatic, and they rejected his message. After Malcolm X spoke of the 1963 assassination of President John F. Kennedy as just the kind of violence that whites had long used against blacks, he was suspended from the Black Muslims. He formed his own group in 1964. However, after he modified his views and agreed that whites and blacks might be able to live together, he was reconverted to the orthodox religion of Islam.

However, the hostility between the militant Black Muslims and those who followed the new Malcolm X had intensified. In 1965, while at a rally in a Harlem ballroom, Malcolm X was shot to death. Three Black Muslims were convicted.

children, four of whom survived. With his wife's money, Muhammad was able to set up a trading business of his own.

When Muhammad was about forty years old, he would often go alone to a cave on Mount Hira to reflect on life. One day a voice came to him saying, "read." But Muhammad could neither read nor write. When the command was repeated, Muhammad left the cave in terror. Once outside, he looked up to see the Angel Gabriel in the form of a man. Gabriel told Muhammad, "You are the Messenger of God." Thereafter, from time to time, the angel reappeared and spoke what Muhammad called revelations, believing them to be messages directly from God. Some forty years later, these revelations were collected and written into the Koran, which is Islam's holy book.

Muhammad recited the revelations to scribes because he could not write them down. Eventually, they were written on clay tablets and other various materials and stored in the home of Muhammad's second wife, Ayesha. Forty followers were given the task of recording these revelations, which became the Koran. Muhammad and many of his followers could recite the Koran by heart, as many Muslims can today. After Muhammad's death, all those who knew the Koran by heart were called together to write the final, authoritative version. Since that time, the Koran has not been changed, not even by a single comma. Strict Muslims even disapprove of translating the Koran into other languages. They believe that only Arabic holds the true meaning of the messages delivered to Muhammad by the angel Gabriel. For that reason, non-Arabic-speaking Muslims try to learn the Arabic language if possible.

As Muhammad preached the truths he received from the angel Gabriel, he gained more and more followers. He was especially popular among the poor

In this artist's depiction, Muhammad is visited by the angel Gabriel, and is delivered the messages that would later become the Koran.

The city of Mecca has been the focal point of Islam for centuries. Here, surrounded by the city's buildings, sits the stone shrine Ka'aba.

since he preached that all people, rich and poor alike, were equal in the eyes of Allah. This did not please the rich people of Mecca, however, who also persecuted Muhammad for preaching a belief in just one God. So, in 622, Muslims began moving out of the city to the more friendly nearby village of Medina. Muhammad himself also moved to Medina in a journey called the *hijrah*. It is from this date that Muslims trace their history.

Besides gaining converts, Muhammad brought law and order to Medina, eventually becoming its leader. But his enemies in Mecca continued to persecute him, and eventually an army from Mecca of some 1,000 men attacked the Muslims at the Battle of Badr. The Muslims, although badly outnumbered, won.

Fighting went on with the people of Mecca for the next several years, with the twice-wounded Muhammad leading his men in battle. In 630, the Muslims were successful and returned to Mecca in triumph. Muhammad removed all idols from the *Ka'aba*, the stone shrine in the center of the city, and it became the center of worship for all Islam, as it remains today.

After Muhammad's death in 632, Arabs continued to spread the word of Islam. This jihad, or so-called holy war was astounding in its success, the main reason being the belief of Muslims that if they were killed in a battle that was fought for Islam, Allah would reward them after death. Most of all, Muslims believed that it was the will of Allah that they should succeed. And succeed they did. Only one hundred years after Muhammad's death, Muslims occupied Spain, Portugal, and all of North Africa. Although most of Christian Europe was untouched, Spain remained under Muslim influence for centuries. By the thirteenth century, Islam had reached China and Southeast Asia. In 1453, the Muslims took Constantinople, the Christian center of the

Byzantine Empire, and renamed it Istanbul. In the seventeenth century, wealthy and powerful Muslim empires existed over much of the known world, including the Ottomans in Turkey. In the twentieth century, however, these empires weakened and disappeared and Islamic influence faded.

The Muslims brought many things other than their faith in the will of Allah to the areas they conquered: advanced methods in medicine, astronomy, and mathematics. Our numbering system is based on arabic numbers.

During the last half of the twentieth century, many countries in the Middle East, such as Iran, Iraq, and Saudi Arabia, had once again come under strict Islamic rule. The rigid dictates of the religion have caused ongoing tension among different Muslim sects, as has the immense wealth that has come to some of these countries through oil production. The volatile political situation in today's Middle East has formed the setting in which Islam must try to find its place in the twenty-first century.

Islam continues to gain thousands of converts to a religious faith that goes beyond spiritual belief. Since Muhammad, Muslims have lived each day of their lives according to key beliefs known as the Five Pillars of Islam—faith, prayer, charity, fasting, and pilgrimage.

The most important pillar is the first—faith. It is based on the belief in Allah as the one and only God. In fact, in order to become a Muslim, a person needs only to stand before two Muslim witnesses and recite a chant called the *shahada*, which declares that there is no God but Allah and that Muhammad is his servant and prophet.

According to the second pillar, prayer, a Muslim must pray five times every day. The times are set (dawn, midday, midafternoon, sunset, and about an hour and a half after sunset) and if possible, Muslims must say these prayers in a mosque, or Muslim

Muslim pilgrims walk great distances during their pilgrimage to Mecca. The fifth pillar of Islam asks that every Muslim try to travel to Mecca during their lifetime.

When Muslims pray daily they are required to turn their faces toward Mecca. Here, pilgrims gather in Mecca around the base of the black stone Ka'aba.

church. Muslims who cannot get to a mosque recite the prayers wherever they are.

The third pillar—charity—requires that Muslims give part of their income to charity each year, and the fourth pillar—fasting—requires that Muslims abstain from eating and drinking between sunrise and sunset during the holy month of Ramadan. At the end of the fasting month, there is a four-day festival during which time presents are exchanged.

The fifth pillar—pilgrimage—is the only one that is not mandatory. It says that every Muslim should try to make at least one trip to Mecca. Every year the approximately two million Muslims who make the journey must follow strict rituals that symbolize the equality of rich or poor before Allah. When they are about six miles away from the sacred city, they must wash and dress simply, the men in white cotton with sandals, the women in a simple dress and head covering. Certain activities such as cutting their hair or picking wildflowers are forbidden.

The pilgrim's objective in the journey to Mecca is the *Ka'aba*, a stone structure about 48 feet high and 52 feet long, covered in black silk, located in the center of the city. Muslims all over the world turn their faces to the *Ka'aba* when saying their daily prayers. A black stone in a corner of the *Ka'aba* is said to date from the time of Adam.

Once in Mecca, Muslims must perform certain duties to complete their pilgrimage. They must walk seven times around the *Ka'aba* in an counterclockwise direction. They must run seven times between the hills of as-Safa and al-Marwah, a tribute to Hagar, an ancestor of the Arab people who ran seven times between these hills looking for water. Pilgrims must also go to the plain of Arafat, about nine miles from Mecca, and spend the afternoon in prayer. From there, pilgrims journey to the plain of Muzadalifah and pick up seventy pebbles, and then travel to the village of Mina, where they throw the pebbles at three pillars, in honor of the prophet Abraham's rejection of the devil. To end their sacred duties in Mecca, Muslims must sacrifice an animal, a goat or sheep—actually, butcher shops do this and give the meat to the poor—and then walk seven times again around the *Ka'aba*.

This religion of Islam clearly asks followers to follow strict rules and customs—from birth until death. Seven days after a child is born, his or her head is shaved and the child is named. In Muslim countries, the weight of the hair in gold and silver should be given to the poor. The Koran says a man may have four wives, although in actual practice, this occurs rarely today. Marriages are often arranged by parents in strictly Muslim countries. Divorce is allowed but frowned upon. When a Muslim dies, his or her body is wrapped in white sheets and placed in a simple grave with the face turned toward Mecca.

Westerners often point to discrimination against women in the Islamic religion. Indeed today, progressive women in some lands with strict Muslim governments have been calling for a relaxing of the old ways. Although Islam says that men and women are equal, a variety of laws seriously curtail a woman's actions. In Saudi Arabia, for instance, women must veil their faces, and they cannot drive cars. In Iran, they must wear the *chador*, a long black gown that covers them from head to toe, in public. Although they can own property and have the right to an education, they may work only if it does not interfere with what is considered their main responsibility—the care of the home.

Certainly, how strictly the rules of Islam are followed depends on the country where one lives. Muslims living in the United States may go about their daily tasks in a far different manner than Muslims living in, for instance, fundamentalist Iran.

Snipes became a convert to Islam while in college and continued practicing the religion while he pursued his acting career. However, in 1988, he modified his position, becoming what he now refers to as a "nonpracticing convert to Islam." Although he continues to have ties with Islam on a spiritual level, he is no longer a formally practicing Muslim.

In 1995 his search for identity led Snipes to join the Million Man March, in Washington. This gathering sought to inspire a new generation of young black men in particular to search for their roots and identity and to strengthen such values as the work ethic, family togetherness, responsibility, and self-respect. March organizers sought to point out that although more Americans have been enjoying financial and educational success, equality for all African Americans is still a long way off. Progress has often been frustratingly slow for young black men who have been the ones who most often exhibit despair and anger. They look around and see hopelessness, and that is exactly the attitude that the Million Man March was formed to change.

Despite its admirable goals, the project has been criticized for the militancy of some of its organizers, most notably Black Muslim leader Louis Farrakhan. But E. Ethelbert Miller, a professor at Howard University in Washington, disagrees. He describes Farrakhan as "dignified." Miller also supports Wesley's position: "The only place you see that dignity today is on screen in *Blade*. You should see the way young black kids react to Wesley Snipes. He's a black superhero."

But others have criticized Snipes for taking part in the march. He was also criticized for attending a speech given by Black Muslim official Khallid Abdul Muhammed and being introduced to the crowd, only days before the Islamic leader was shot. Responding to questions about the actor's stand on race relations

Two men greet each other with smiles during 1995's Million Man March, which Wesley attended to show his solidarity with fellow African-American men.

by his presence at such events, a spokesman for Snipes offers this comment: "Wesley has a Jewish agent, a Jewish lawyer, and a gay publicist. If he was really aligning himself with what this guy [meaning Khallid Abdul Muhammed] was saying, he'd put a bullet in each of us."

Perhaps Wesley's existing connection with his chosen religion is best expressed in the name of his production company, Amen Ra—which translates as "an unseen source of all creation." He defines himself as an "African spiritualist" who was raised in the Baptist church as well as a practicing Muslim for ten years. "My spirit," he concludes. "I think that's the only way I've been able to survive."

5

START THE CAMERAS

— ◊ —

Wesley and Annabella Sciorra embrace during a scene from Jungle Fever, one of many high-profile projects Wesley worked on as his star rose in Hollywood.

WESLEY SNIPES HIT the Big Apple in 1984, a young man newly converted to the faith of Islam and with a brand new diploma making him a "certified actor." Despite his impressive acting training, competition was fierce and no one was particularly impressed with Wesley. As with many other young aspiring actors, the only work he could get was parking cars, and, as he is quick to add, installing telephones and giving therapeutic massages. He describes his work at Columbia University in New York as a parking attendant: "I thought I was going to make some extra money with tips. Unfortunately, I worked in the teachers' parking lot. They didn't tip. They were as poor as me."

Snipes soon had additional reasons to be concerned about making money. In 1985, he married April, a young woman whom he met while at college. Even though they both worked, it was difficult to make ends meet. Wesley's teacher Karen Rugerio remembers that time too, for she and Wesley kept in touch. Whenever he and April went down to Florida to see his family, they visited her. She says, "When they felt like Italian food, they came to my house."

Then in 1986 a break came on the scene for Wesley. A casting director who had seen him in a college production got him a small part in the motion picture *Wildcats*, a zany comedy about a football-crazy physical education teacher (Goldie Hawn) who gets to coach a varsity team in a tough urban neighborhood. Snipes was cast as Trumaine, also called First and Goal, one of her players. April also got a small part in the cast.

His next acting role was in *The Boys of Winter*, an off-Broadway play by John Pielmeier. Snipes played one of the soldiers suffering from the ravaging effects of the war in Vietnam. From there, he appeared in Wole Soyinka's *Death and the King's Horsemen* at Lincoln Center. His next part was on Broadway at last, but it was a dramatic switch that required him to don spike heels to play drag queen Sister Boom-Boom in *Execution of Justice*. Snipes's extensive dancer's training, caught the eye of producer Emily Mann, who thought he was wonderful. "I had never seen a man put on high heels and walk that way. That guy is going to be a star!"

His dancer's training and martial arts skills helped him land another movie role. In *Streets of Gold* (1986), he plays Roland Jenkins, a cocky black boxer and one of two young men training for the U.S. boxing team under the eye of a former Russian boxing champ. After that film, nothing much happened and he had to go back to parking cars. The next year he won a small part as the ambulance driver in *Critical Condition*, the Richard Pryor comedy about a con artist who takes charge of a prison hospital. The film didn't get very good reviews, but the exposure he received proved important in Snipes's young career and allowed him to be seen by the "right" people. In this case, the right person was Spike Lee, a young African American on his way to becoming a highly acclaimed and controversial director whose films were taking a harsh look at American racism.

Snipes had a small role that year in *Bad*, a Michael Jackson video in which he plays a tough

Spike Lee often looked to Wesley to fill important roles in his films, although Wesley passed on a part in Lee's Do the Right Thing.

gang leader who shoves Jackson up against a wall. He did it so well that Lee thought Snipes must have scared Jackson half to death.

Next came *Vietnam War Story 2*, the second part of a made-for-cable movie trilogy about the emotional effects of the war on U.S. soldiers. Based on the real-life experiences of the men who were there, the terrible conflicts of war are relived in three short stories, "An Old Ghost Walks the Earth," the "R&R," and "The Fragging." For his performance, Snipes won the 1989 ACE Award for the best actor in a made-for-cable movie. At last, he was starting to get some recognition.

It was at this point that Spike Lee offered Snipes a part in *Do the Right Thing*, his upcoming film about racial tensions in Brooklyn. Snipes turned Lee down so that he could take a larger role in *Major League* (1989), a comedy in which he plays Willie Mays Hays, a talented but undisciplined baseball player who can run like the wind but can't hit the ball. Hays is just one of the oddballs in this story of a baseball franchise owner who wants to get out of her contract by organizing a team that's guaranteed to lose games and fans. Of course, the lovable misfits—improbably—win the pennant!

Just as his career was starting to move, changes began to occur in Wesley's personal life. He and April had a son they named Jelani Asar. Unfortunately, the marriage did not last, and they were divorced in 1990. Snipes was devastated that his marriage had ended after so few years. "My dad left when I was two, and I was doing the same thing to my son," he said. "When I got married, I believed you weren't a man until you were capable of managing a family." He continued, "I was going to prove to everybody—all these people who say a successful black man can't have a lasting relationship—that I could."

This sad experience was unhappily far from unique, especially in the high pressure, glitzy entertainment world, where young attractive people meet, fall in love, marry, have a child, and then realize it was all too much too soon. "We married thinking we could change each other," Snipes said. He said that when he left the household, he felt he had lost everything. He drove around at night, sleeping in his car, and dropping in at the homes of friends to change clothes.

The only answer seemed to be work. His next movie was *King of New York* (1990), in which he had a small but well-reviewed part as Thomas Flanigan, a tough cop who helps to bring down a powerful, charismatic drug lord.

That same year, Snipes appeared in *H.E.L.P.*— Harlem Eastside Lifesaving Program—a TV action-adventure series in which he played New York police officer Lou Barton. Broadcast on HBO for one month, it featured policemen, firefighters, and medics coping with crisis after crisis against a backdrop of New York City, where it was filmed.

Once again, Spike Lee sent an offer, and this time Snipes accepted it. *Mo' Better Blues* (1990), the first film about jazz by a black director, tells the story of

Wesley as jazz saxophonist Shadow Henderson in Spike Lee's Mo' Better Blues.

a brilliant but self-centered jazz trumpeter named Bleek Gilliam, played by Denzel Washington. He is bitter about the second-class status of jazz musicians in the black community and indifferent to the lives and feelings of his two girlfriends. His rival, both in music and romance, is a jazz saxophonist, Shadow Henderson, played by Snipes. Henderson believes that he can attract a black audience to the clubs by experimenting with jazz and pop music.

The movie did not get much praise from the critics, but they did single out both Washington and Snipes for their work. *Rolling Stone* thought that Snipes gave the most "arresting performance," and the *Village Voice* complimented Snipes on how "comfortable" he looked on the bandstand. He should have. For this role, Snipes had watched endless tapes of jazz legends such as John Coltrane and

Wesley played a ruthless drug dealer, Nino Brown, in the film New Jack City. *The film received critical accolades for its grim portrayal of crime and drug addiction and was a hit with audiences.*

memorized the fingering for all of the music played in the film.

Word was soon getting around Hollywood about a handsome, charismatic young actor named Wesley Snipes. In fact, inspired by memories of Snipes in the video *Bad*, screenwriter Barry Michael Cooper created the character of Nino Brown, the ruthless drug lord of Harlem's crack-cocaine trade in *New Jack City*

(1991), a film in which Wesley Snipes was at last to have the leading role.

New Jack City, the first directing effort by actor and screenwriter Mario Van Peebles, tells the brutal story of Nino Brown, a businessman and gangster, who transforms the corner drug-dealing operations of Harlem into a slick modern-day enterprise. Like the dictator of a small country, he commands an army of well-equipped enforcers who do his bidding and keep the operation running smoothly. Snipes said he was able to draw upon his years growing up in the Bronx for the ruthless, pent-up energy of Brown. Critics likened his portrayal of the swaggering, scary Brown to such triumphs as the one-and-only Edward G. Robinson playing a small-time hood turned big-time gangster in *Little Caesar* (1930), or the great Paul Muni as an Al Capone–like mobster in *Scarface* (1932).

Trial scene from New Jack City. *Wesley drew upon his experiences growing up in the Bronx to help define the character of Nino Brown.*

New Jack City opened in March 1991 and earned more than $22 million at the box office in just three weeks. Such was the growing power of Snipes's name on screen. However, the opening was clouded by violent outbursts and looting that occurred after showings in New York City, Chicago, Las Vegas, and Los Angeles. Critics blamed the violence of the film itself. Snipes was adamant in denying the charge. Claiming that the movie was clearly against drugs and against violence, he and others blamed the outbursts on the fact that movie houses had oversold tickets when the film opened and had to turn patrons away. In fact, Snipes was indignant about the fans' violent reactions and felt that teenagers

Wesley once again teamed up with director Spike Lee on the film Jungle Fever, *which deals with a black man's struggles with marriage, adultery, and interracial relationships.*

seemed to have gotten the wrong idea about who were the good guys and the bad guys. About the oversold tickets, he said, "They oversold the showings by 1,500 tickets and the theater owners didn't give the money back. The same thing would happen with a Menudo concert or the Rolling Stones." After all the furor quieted down, however, *New Jack City* went on to become highly successful and boosted Snipes's career another notch. The actor was on a roll. That same year he played a totally different leading man in another Spike Lee film, *Jungle Fever*. In this, he assumes the role of Flipper Purify, an upper-middle-class architect living in Harlem with his wife and child and aspiring to become the first black partner in his firm. Despite his happy marriage, he becomes involved in an affair with his white secretary, a liaison doomed because of the cultural differences between the two and their families. The film was cited as a vehicle for Spike Lee's views on interracial relationships, but Snipes later said he believed it was about how color conscious American society really is.

Roles were coming more easily now and Snipes was busy. In 1992, he appeared in three films—*White Men Can't Jump, The Waterdance,* and *Passenger 57*—that went a long way toward landing his feet in the Hollywood Walk of Fame. In *White Men Can't Jump*, a top moneymaker, Snipes plays Sidney Deane, an out-of-work roofer in Los Angeles. To support his family, he hustles basketball games at an outdoor court. His partner in this venture is a white guy named Billy Hoyle, played by Woody Harrelson of *Cheers* fame. Problems ensue because Billy once backed out on a deal with the mob to throw a college basketball game. The film received generally good reviews, but the chemistry between Snipes and Harrelson got raves.

In *The Waterdance*, Snipes showed his versatility as a top actor in a story that centers on a multiethnic rehabilitation center where a young novelist has been admitted after a hiking accident leaves him paralyzed. Snipes is Raymond Hill, one of the patients, a smart-talker who must face not only

Wesley's training as an athlete and dancer proved very useful in the filming of White Men Can't Jump.

Wesley developed a strong on-screen chemistry with his fellow star of White Men Can't Jump, *Woody Harrelson.*

his new limitations but the fact that his marriage is falling apart, due mainly to his unfaithfulness in the past. The movie won several awards in 1992 at the Sundance Film Festival, and Snipes was singled out for his rich portrayal. For the role, he visited numerous rehabilitation centers to understand a wheelchair patient's physical problems and to gain insight into the emotional trauma that the disabled person suffers.

In *Passenger 57*, Snipes plays a cool action hero, John Cutter, an airline security guard and martial arts expert. On a flight to Los Angeles, he suddenly finds himself in the middle of a hijacking, by an internationally known criminal and his pals.

It is worth a closer look at *Passenger 57* to see Wesley Snipes playing the action hero to the fullest.

As John Cutter, Snipes is the best airline security expert in the business. He is thinking about retirement, mostly because he can't get over the memory of a recent holdup, which he tried to stop and during which his beloved wife was killed. But Cutter's boss convinces him to take an important job in Los Angeles.

Snipes winds up on an airliner to L.A. that is hijacked by a gang of ruthless criminals. In an effort to subdue them, Snipes uses some of his martial arts skills, knocking one hijacker down with a clean kick. After causing the plane to lose fuel and nearly crash-land, Snipes escapes while the aircraft is still rolling—again, using his martial arts skills to roll lightly to the ground.

During the rest of the film, which covers efforts to free the airline passengers and capture the criminals—successfully, of course!—Snipes gets involved in some hair-raising episodes. In general, he is always one step ahead of the bad guys, all the while looking quite dashing, sporting one silver earring. John Cutter, a.k.a. Wesley Snipes, is one cool guy.

But, of course, that's what action flicks are all about. Cool heroes and nonstop energy. From opening

Wesley Snipes in his role as John Cutter in Passenger 57.

credits until the end, the pace never slows. The hero gets in scrape after scrape, and no matter how impossible it seems, the hero will always win—eventually!

Wesley Snipes is not the first black actor in Hollywood to become an action hero, although it's not that common either. Eddie Murphy, for instance, although well known for such roles, usually throws in a good deal of comedy as well. And superstar Denzel Washington has generally avoided action films entirely.

Black actors making a name for themselves in this type of movie include Richard Roundtree, who found instant stardom in 1971 as the hip hero of *Shaft*, in which he plays a private eye hired to find the kidnapped daughter of a Harlem drug lord. Although critics liked Roundtree in this and the film's two sequels in 1972 and 1973, they were unhappy with the extreme violence. He has since played supporting parts in several films and has appeared on television as well.

Another black action hero was Jim Brown, an All-American football hero at Syracuse University and star fullback for the Cleveland Browns from 1957 to 1967. Handsome and brooding, he appeared in such action films as *The Dirty Dozen* (1967), a World War II action movie, and *Slaughter* (1972), in which Brown plays an ex-Green Beret of the Vietnam era who goes after the syndicate that kills his parents.

Carl Weathers made an instant name for himself as the brawny heavyweight champion Apollo Creed in the *Rocky* movies (1976, 1979, 1982, 1985) with Sylvester Stallone. He continued making films into the 1990s.

During 1993, the up-and-coming Wesley Snipes appeared in three more films: *Boiling Point*, *Rising Sun*, and *Demolition Man*. In *Boiling Point*, the first one-million-dollar role for Snipes, the actor plays

Jimmy Mercer, a burned-out FBI agent who is hot on the trail of the man who killed his colleague and friend during a sting operation. Although most critics found it entertaining, Snipes's performance was not as well received.

Snipes costarred with Sean Connery in *Rising Sun*, a film based on the best-selling novel by Michael Crichton. Snipes plays Web Smith, an inexperienced L.A. cop working with worldly detective Connery, who is an expert on Japan. They investigate a homicide that occurs during the opening of a new Japanese-owned office building in the city. Soon, they are involved with a U.S. sena-

While Wesley was playing black action heroes seriously, the 1998 film I'm Gonna Git You Sucka *poked fun at the related "blaxploitation" genre of the 1970s. From left: Bernie Casey, Keenen Ivory Wayans, Jim Brown.*

tor, a Japanese corporation, and a Japanese mobster. The reviews of the film were mixed—some thinking it was a good murder mystery; some thought that it was confusing and anti-Japanese. New for Snipes was the slight comic touch he brought to his role as the sometimes bewildered young cop. Not everyone liked that either, although most did feel that Snipes held his own playing against the far more experienced Connery.

Snipes took on superstar Sylvester Stallone in *Demolition Man*, an action comedy about the future. Snipes dyed his hair blond to play Simon Phoenix, a dangerous criminal who escapes during a parole hearing after spending thirty-six years being frozen in a "cryogenic" prison. The year is 2032, and society is peaceful, extremely orderly, and against violence. Because leaders in megalopolis "San Angeles" do not know how to cope with the excessively violent Phoenix, they unfreeze his old enemy, Los Angeles police sergeant John Spartan, played by Stallone. Spartan, who is as violent in his way as Phoenix, had also been frozen in 1996. Together, the two manage nearly to wreck the city of the future. Critics thought the film was surprisingly funny but extremely violent.

Although critics acknowledged Snipes's talent and polished movements in action sequences, they began to decry the excessive use of violence in his movies—a forceful objection to the work of a man who himself often said "violence is disgusting." Indeed, at times it did seem as though Snipes was setting a poor role model for his growing number of young fans. Then, in an unfortunate case of life imitating art, things began to slide in Wesley's real life.

While filming *Demolition Man* in Los Angeles, Snipes often rode his motorcycle to the set and around the city. On one such trip, he lost control of the bike and overturned. Although he was not badly injured, witnesses told police that they had spotted a gun under the actor's jacket. Snipes was charged with two criminal misdemeanors: one for carrying a concealed weapon—a semiautomatic pistol bought in Florida and registered in California—and one for carrying a loaded weapon. He was released with a $1,000 fine and a six-month jail term on each count. Later represented by an attorney in court, Snipes pleaded no contest to the charge of carrying a loaded weapon. In return for the plea, the concealed weapons charge was dropped. He was given two years' unsupervised probation and fined $2,700.

The early 1990s were a mixture of success as well as turmoil for actor Wesley Snipes. Films that were

Wesley played the diabolical villain Simon Phoenix in Demolition Man. *The film was very violent, and some critics wondered how Wesley could explain his role given his often-stated view that "violence is disgusting."*

moneymakers but not always well reviewed, trouble with the law, trouble with marriage ending in divorce, a split-up family. The seemingly charmed life was eluding him. It was time to slow down and take a good look at himself.

6
SHIFTING GEARS

T O STOP HIS life from spinning out of control, Snipes turned to his career with renewed determination. As he says, "I knew that I still had to perfect my craft. I had to do the work."

And work he did. *Drop Zone* (1994) took him back in the action flick category in the role of Pete Nessip, a U.S. marshal running after some skydiving bad guys in this story of undercover drug agents and international narcotics dealers. Critics weren't crazy about the plot but admired the dazzling film sequences. Also in 1994, he played Roemello Skuggs in *Sugar Hill*, a film about a black American family in turmoil in a once quiet, refined Harlem neighborhood. Snipes is a drug lord who has to care for his junkie father and epileptic brother, all the while trying to get out of his dangerous trade. Of the violence in this movie, Snipes commented, "It should make people uncomfortable and give them a sense of the horror of living a life like that."

Three movies came out in 1995 featuring Snipes in leading roles. In *Money Train*, he was paired again with his old pal Woody Harrelson, in an action film about New York City transit cops who argue over everything and get involved in the theft of a city subway car. Critics thought the two stars were funny but had adverse comments about the excessive violence. But Snipes's other two film roles that year moved in a

In a departure from his action-star roles, Wesley wore women's clothing in To Wong Foo, Thanks for Everything, Julie Newmar. *He is seen here with costars John Leguizamo and Patrick Swayze.*

Wesley once again worked with Woody Harrelson in the action/comedy Money Train, *which also featured another rising star, singer and actress Jennifer Lopez.*

new direction. He appeared in *Waiting to Exhale*, but took no credits at all, wanting the female stars, including Whitney Houston, to get the focus in this tale of four black women who can't seem to find decent men in their lives. In *To Wong Foo, Thanks for Everything, Julie Newmar*, Snipes steps back into his high heels. He plays Noxeema Jackson in this story of three drag queens heading for Hollywood when their car breaks down in a small town. Critics found the film tiresome.

In 1996, Snipes began to shift the focus of his roles. In *The Fan*, he plays Bobby Rayburn, the new baseball star of the San Francisco Giants who is being pursued by "fan" Robert De Niro, a guy on the edge, a loser with an unhealthy passion for the Giants and an obsession with their newest star. Snipes was frustrated with the film because he was tired of playing muscular cops and super athletes and had wanted to play the "psycho" De Niro role. He wanted to return to his dramatic roots. He lamented that people didn't yet understand that he was a dramatically trained actor first and an action hero second. Still, he understood that he was probably too young looking to be cast as a man who'd been through the trials of life. "But I'm a patient man," Snipes said. "I can wait."

In *One Night Stand* (1997), Snipes plays Max Carlyle, a TV commercial director. A happily married man whose business life is also going well, he uncharacteristically falls for a white woman he meets by chance. Unlike the situation in *Jungle Fever*, nothing is made of the interracial aspects of the relationship, including the fact that Snipes's wife is not black but Asian American. Snipes reflected on the various aspects of the film by saying that the story is about "self-reflection and responsibility and friendship," not interracial relationships. It is also about faithfulness, marriage, and personal change, and it won Snipes a best actor nod at the Venice Film Festival.

Refusing to be typecast: Wesley as a drag queen in To Wong Foo, Thanks for Everything, Julie Newmar.

In The Fan, *Robert De Niro (above) plays a psychotic fan who is obsessed with a major league baseball star, played by Wesley Snipes (opposite page).*

Although Snipes had some doubts about the basic premises of the movie—perhaps because of his own failed marriage, he wasn't so sure about the idea of falling in love at first sight—he did want the chance to work with Mike Figgis, who directed the Oscar-winning Nicolas Cage in *Leaving Las Vegas*. (Actually, Cage was tapped for this role too, but he refused because he had just gotten married and didn't want to play the part of a cheating husband.)

In 1997 Snipes also appeared in *Murder at 1600*, a thriller and action film, in which he plays Harlan Regis, a Washington, D.C., homicide detective called in to investigate a murder when a White House staffer is found dead in an Oval Office bathroom. Assorted cover-ups and intrigue follow as the many agencies connected to the White House try to protect their own.

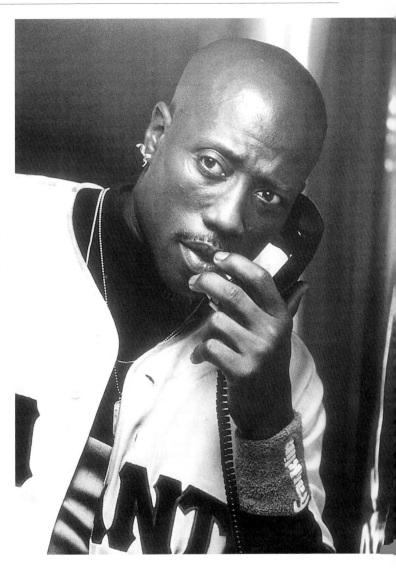

"These kinds of roles are few and far between for an actor as young as myself," Snipes said at the time. "The thrill is more intellectual." Does Snipes throw himself into his work? Costar Diane Lane thinks so. She said of his performance, "He's so earnest he could pass a lie-detector test." According to *E!Online* critic Bob Strauss, "If any actor can convince an audience that a Washington, D.C., homicide cop is capable of saving the president, preserving democracy, and ensuring world peace—all while solving the Murder at 1600—it's Wesley Snipes."

The year 1998 was a big one for Snipes's career—three films that drew some serious attention and good reviews for his performances. One was *Down in the Delta*, a story set in rural Mississippi, although mostly filmed near Toronto, Canada. Snipes costarred and, through his company Amen Ra, coproduced this film, which was directed by acclaimed poet Maya Angelou. The film tells the tale of a troubled single mother from Chicago, played by Alfre Woodard, whose life is a mess. With her two children, she takes a bus back to her roots in Mississippi to spend the summer. She lives with relatives and works in their chicken restaurant as she tries to put her life back together with the help of the cast of characters, among them Will, played by Snipes.

When the movie opened at the Toronto Film Festival, a frustrated Snipes said that it took him more than four years to get the project going. Producers were concerned about the racial aspects in the United States. Said Snipes, "The film transcends cultural boundaries as well as politics. . . . it is fundamentally about compassion and family and respect."

U.S. Marshals saw Tommy Lee Jones return as the take-charge marshal from *The Fugitive* (1993), which won six Oscars. Jones, playing the character that also won him an Oscar, and his team are on the trail of Snipes, playing the role of crafty criminal and fugitive, Mark Sheridan, a C.I.A. operative who is accused of killing two Secret Service agents. Snipes said it was a great challenge to play "a man whose job it is to assassinate people. He's been trained to be a shadow warrior." This three-star action thriller was voted by the critics as highly entertaining.

Then came *Blade*, a sci-fi horror epic. Snipes certainly put his martial arts training to work here. He

plays Blade, the part-human, part-vampire hero based on a character created for Marvel Comics by Marv Wolfman. In this ninety-minute flick cited for its gore, Blade goes after a megalomaniac who is out to control the world.

With Angela Bassett in the 1995 hit Waiting to Exhale.

In 1997, Snipes presented his voice, but not the rest of him, for an HBO animated musical family series entitled *Happily Ever After: Fairy Tales for Every Child*. Children of different races participate in the retelling of thirteen classic fairy tales. Behind the cartoon characters are the voices of many famous entertainers, including Whoopi Goldberg, Denzel Washington, Rosie Perez, Jimmy Smits, and Wesley Snipes, who gave his voice to the character of the Pied Piper.

When Snipes comes out from behind the voice in a production, it has generally included showing off some martial arts training, as he did in *Blade*. Even in a film that does not call for action heroes, he is a very

A film crew uses a steady-cam to shoot a scene from U.S. Marshals in which Tommy Lee Jones and Wesley Snipes exit a courthouse.

physical performer, acutely aware of his body. Some of this stems from his natural ability and training as a dancer, some from his long years of study and training in martial arts. Since his mother first enrolled him in a class in the Bronx to help him learn to defend himself, his interest has continued.

What are the martial arts? To enter this field means to discipline not just the body but the mind and spirit as well. True martial artists use these skills only for protection, not as aggressors. The martial arts teach skills of self-defense and concentration. They are also a great way to get in shape.

The martial arts trace their beginnings to Asia some 1,500 years ago. An Indian monk named Bodhidharma, a restless and wealthy young man, set out alone on a walking journey from India to China. He wanted to tell people about his search for peace and happiness, which he found through meditation and a

As a vengeful, determined vampire hunter in the 1998 film Blade.

The martial arts have helped keep Wesley in good shape, enabling him to take on physically demanding roles like that of a basketball hustler in White Men Can't Jump.

new philosophy that came to be called Ch'an by the Chinese and Zen by the Japanese.

Bodhidharma finally reached China in what is now Henan Province. At first the monks he encountered thought he was crazy, but eventually he began to teach them to meditate. But at the end of many hours of meditation, the monks were stiff and sore, so Bodhidharma began instructions in physical exercises as well. Eventually, the monks got themselves in very good physical shape, and they could stand in one position for long periods of time without moving. They could also punch and kick the air with alarming swiftness and power, new skills that they used only for self-defense. Eventually, the monks became known for their physical talents and word of this developing martial art began to spread across China and Asia. By the end of the twentieth century, there were 400 different styles of martial arts just in China alone.

The martial arts came to the United States after World War II. U.S. servicemen who had been in Japan came home talking about this interesting and powerful form of self-discipline and defense. Today, most of the hundreds of different styles of martial arts that are taught in the United States share certain characteristics. Training classes usually begin and end with a bow, and sometimes a meditation period begins each class. The two key movements in the martial arts are the

BRUCE LEE, KING OF THE MARTIAL ARTS

Bruce Lee—the actor who introduced American moviegoers to the martial arts—grew up in Hong Kong and later came to the United States with his family. Only five feet eight inches tall and weighing about 145 pounds, he was a skilled and impressive fighter. His skills landed him the role of Kato, a bodyguard on the *Green Hornet* television show.

Lee stayed in Hollywood after the show ended, although acting jobs were hard to get for a young Chinese man. But in 1972, a lead role was created for him in *Kung Fu*, a television series set in the American West. Lee was shocked, however, when the part went to white actor David Carradine. But Lee's big break came in 1973 with *Return of the Dragon*, which featured a big fight scene between Lee and new action star Chuck Norris. Not long after, while filming *Game of Death*, Lee died suddenly at the age of thirty-two. Brain swelling was cited as the cause, and some mystery still remains about the tragedy. In 1994, there was talk of a curse on Lee's family because his son Brandon, also a martial arts expert, was shot to death while on the set of *The Crow*. The blank bullets shot at him during the filming somehow turned out to be real. Years after his death, Bruce Lee remains a top name in martial arts.

There are many different styles of the martial arts, but they all have a few qualities in common: discipline, nonaggression, and respect for one's opponent.

hand strike and the kick. The most common hand strike is the punch, formed by rolling the fingers up tightly. The skillful martial artist can deliver many different types of punches without being physically very strong. The different kicking techniques are delivered from a distance of several feet from the side, or front, or in a circular move. The most important quality in the delivery of a kick is surprise!

Despite the many different styles of martial arts, most share two goals—peace and spiritual development.

Of the many styles of martial arts, the two with which American youngsters are probably most familiar are judo and ninja. Judo means "gentle way." It's really more of a sport than a method of self-defense. In the late 1800s, the kicks and punches of jujutsu, a Japanese art of self-defense, were used to create judo. Since 1972, judo has been included as an Olympic sport.

The art of ninja began centuries ago. The ninja—whose fighting skills were legendary— served as bodyguards for the famed samurai. They could do amazing things such as escape from being tied with ropes to a tree or stay underwater for many hours using just a tiny bamboo reed to breathe, and they were very skilled with many weapons. Ninjas also flung nets over their enemies, climbed walls with spikes strapped to hands and feet, and rolled themselves into tight balls to avoid being spotted in the middle of a field. The art of the ninja has largely died out except for the interest generated by the Teenage Mutant Ninja Tutles in movies and on television.

Wesley Snipes excels in yet another type of martial arts—*capoeira*, a theatrical and acrobatic variation brought to Brazil by African slaves in the sixteenth century. Put to work on farmlands, the slaves practiced in whatever spare time was given them what looked to outsiders as an innocent, colorful dance. To the sounds

Two individuals perform capoeira on stage. Snipes excels at this highly acrobatic form of martial arts that combines elements of fighting and dancing.

of happy music, the Africans practiced kicks and leg locks that looked much like movements in a circus. The slaveowners might not have been amused had they realized that what they were seeing was a fight dance. These kicks and leg locks, when done correctly, had the potential to be deadly killers.

It is interesting to note that the slaves who practiced this martial art concentrated on headstands and kicks rather than anything that involved the arms. Why? Because it was not uncommon at the time to discipline a slave for some major infraction by cutting off his arm. If that happened, the slave trained in capoeira could still fight and defend himself.

This style of martial arts spread throughout Brazil, especially among the poorer people. But the government grew fearful of those who could defend themselves so skillfully, and declared capoeira illegal in Brazil around the turn of the twentieth century. The police tried to destroy all training centers, but some survived, as did the skill.

Today this martial art form is still outlawed in some parts of Brazil, although the first legal training school was opened in the country in 1932. Capoeira has spread beyond Brazil, taught all over the world, mainly by Brazilians, as a sport and also as a way to keep in shape. Its movements are distinctive—from spinning headstands, similar to those seen in American break dancing, to intricate dance steps and cartwheels, all of which are accompanied by music. In fact, learning to play an instrument and to sing along are part of the training for capoeira students.

Wesley Snipes has thus had the opportunity to use his skills in capoeira and martial arts training in his work. When you are watching his action films, you thus have a chance to see the real thing!

7

THE MAN BEHIND
THE ACTOR

—— ❦ ——

WESLEY SNIPES IS a talented, handsome actor with a graceful dancer's body who modestly says he does not believe himself to be particularly good looking. However, he adds, "I've got a little something going on, a little something. . . . What I may be lacking in looks, I make up for in personality and experience. And tricks. I know a lot of tricks. When you hang in the shadows a little bit, you pick up all the other stuff."

Snipes is also a fashion-conscious man. Even if he weren't recognized as a movie star, he would turn heads in a crowd just for his headgear. He likes to show up at a movie premiere or social event wearing the most flamboyant of toppers! His displays of jewelry and evening attire also turn heads. For the opening of *To Wong Foo, Thanks for Everything! Julie Newmar*, he arrived in a flowing cape and turban-like headgear. Snipes says he dresses the way he feels and shrugs off much being made of his interest in fashion. "One year you're part of the fifty most beautiful people, and the next year, you're on the worst-dressed list." In fact, Snipes was voted one of the fifty most beautiful people in the world by *People* magazine in 1991.

Snipes admits to an interest in women's fashions, too. He admires well-dressed women and likes to be seen with them. "I'm a romantic kind of guy," he says.

Wesley Snipes depends as much on his charming personality and wit as he does on his good looks and style. Here he hams it up with a photographer during an appearance at the opening of a new Planet Hollywood.

"I like the whole idea of courting a woman and bringing her flowers."

But what of romance itself? Snipes has some definite ideas about that, too. Having dated mostly black women, he says this has sometimes been a difficult experience. He feels that all black people have been wounded and that leaves scars. "We're a wounded people and we want to possess and we want to own. We don't want to compromise." Although he has been dating restaurant owner Donna Wong, an Asian American, for some time, Snipes says they are not ready for marriage.

In his high-profile, show biz world, Snipes has not forgotten his family—particularly his son, Jelani, whom the actor calls "precocious." The boy lives in Brooklyn with his mother. Snipes also maintains a home nearby so that he can see the boy whenever he is in town. How does Snipes deal with the fact that he left his son as his own father had left him? Sometimes he admits to feeling regret that he has been a less than ideal father. Snipes said that his father was not there for most of his growing-up years, although he would visit young Wesley from time to time. It wasn't until Snipes graduated from college that he realized what the loss had meant to him, and he is determined that will not happen to Jelani.

"I absolutely make it a point to see him whenever I can," Snipes says. "The most important thing I can teach him is knowledge of self—to know who he is." Snipes says he has already spent more time with his boy than his own father spent with him. "I know that as long as I take advantage of the opportunities I have to be with him, he'll want to be with me. That's what's important to me."

Wesley also remains very close to his mother, who goes to all his movies and is distressed if the critics write negative reviews about them. But she's gotten used to bad press and realizes that there will be ups and downs in the life of a professional actor.

Wesley appears at the premiere of his film The Art of War *with his current love interest, Donna Wong. Wesley finds that relationships can be difficult with his hectic career as an actor.*

Snipes is grateful to his mother for his upbringing, for keeping him focused and in line. "I feared the wrath of Marian," he says with a laugh. "My mom was no fake. She still isn't."

Whenever possible, Snipes spends time with his family in Orlando. He built a house for his mother in the Orlando area, and wanted to do the same for his grandmother, Nana Ruth, but she wanted to stay in the old homestead. So Snipes had the house remodeled and now Nana fishes off the dock of her refurbished home. Says Karen Rugerio, Snipes's former high school teacher, "These are two strong women who raised a very fine young man. He's with them a lot. They even went with him when he was a guest on the *Jay Leno* show."

Snipes sees his younger sister Brigette when he visits the family as well. A former security worker, she is married and lives in Orlando.

In addition to his son and family in Florida, Snipes remembers his roots by helping others. He attends seminars at SUNY in Purchase and Jones High School in Orlando when he can. He conducts workshops for aspiring actors and sometimes even uses them as extras in his films to give them experience and exposure. His charitable foundation helps kids in New York and Chicago to overcome the bonds of poverty and move on.

Wesley Snipes has come a long way from life in the South Bronx. Carolyn Pincus, one of his teachers in elementary school, confesses that she was, back then, a little concerned about Snipes. "He was so bright," she says. "He had so many options. I just knew he was going to be a judge or stand in front of the judge!" Snipes, as we know, did neither and managed instead to become a high-profile celebrity, who owns homes in Los Angeles, New York, and Florida. He is one of an elite group of powerful black actors in Hollywood commanding $10 million for a movie.

So, where does Wesley Snipes go from here? He says that he has always tried to be practical about his career. Very versatile, he does not hesitate to play roles that were not written for black actors. He understands the problems that many black actors face. "You will never hear me say I don't see myself as a black actor, but just an actor who happens to be black. Every chance I get, I am going to tell you I'm an African-American man who is acting."

He takes his career very seriously and continues to expand, to perfect his craft. He says he wants to be twice as good and twice as fast, to be able to change personalities and be fully committed and believable. He also sees writing and directing movies in his future, although he plans to continue to star in them

Wesley takes a moment to chat with his costar from The Art of War, *Marie Matiko. In the film, his character is framed for the death of a Chinese ambassador.*

During 2001 Wesley worked on a sequel to Blade. He seems to be thriving as one of Hollywood's most sought-after actors for a new wave of action films.

for a long time. His own California-based production company, Amen Ra, produces movies and TV projects.

Snipes started out the new century with one of his tried-and-true formulas, an action film. This one is *The Art of War*, in which he costars with Anne Archer and Donald Sutherland. Where does he go from here?

"I'm blessed to be in the right place at the right time," he admits. "I'm just thankful that I realized acting is what I'm supposed to be doing." Snipes also knows how fickle the public's interest can be, and he realizes there is always the possibility of overexposure or even burnout. But he seems able to deal with the situation: "I try to schedule the work in a way where it doesn't drain on me too much." He also wants people to see him in a range of dramatic roles. He knows that probably a majority of moviegoers associate him with his action films, not for roles such as Max Carlyle in *One Night Stand*. Max is a man who has come to a point in his life where he must make choices, what Snipes describes as the winter that is part of everyone's life.

If Max Carlyle is in the winter of his life, Snipes must be in the spring of his as far as his career is concerned. For sure, where there's Wesley Snipes, actor and man behind the actor, as his character in *Blade* says, "There's work to be done."

CHRONOLOGY

—— ✿ ——

1962   Wesley Snipes born in Orlando, Florida, on July 31.

1963   After divorcing Wesley's father, his mother moves family to Bronx, New York.

1969   Enrolls in martial arts classes at Harlem YMCA.

1974   Has first stage role in an off-Broadway production, *The Me Nobody Knows*.

1975   Enters High School for the Performing Arts in New York City.

1976   Family moves back to Orlando.

1980   Graduates from Jones High in Orlando; accepted into theater arts program at the State University of New York (SUNY), Purchase.

1981–1982 Becomes interested in religion of Islam.

1984   Graduates from SUNY; moves to New York City.

1985   Marries April, whom he met at SUNY; plays in *The Boys of Winter*, *Death and the King's Horsemen*, and *Execution of Justice*.

1986   Appears in *Wildcats* and *Streets of Gold*.

1987   Appears in *Critical Condition*.

1988   Modifies his adherence to Islam.

1989   Appears in *Vietnam War Story* and *Major League*.

1990   Is divorced; ex-wife and son, Jelani Asar, move to Brooklyn, where Snipes buys a home; appears in *King of New York* and *Mo' Better Blues*.

1991   Appears in *New Jack City* and *Jungle Fever*.

1992   Appears in *White Men Can't Jump*, *The Waterdance*, and *Passenger 57*.

1993   Appears in *Boiling Point*, *Rising Sun*, and *Demolition Man*; pleads no contest to charge of carrying a concealed weapon after motorcycle accident; receives two years' probation and a fine.

1994   Appears in *Drop Zone* and *Sugar Hill*.

1995   Appears in *Money Train*, *Waiting to Exhale*, and *To Wong Foo, Thanks for Everything! Julie Newmar*; joins Million Man March in Washington, D.C.

1996   Appears in *The Fan*.

1997   Appears in *One Night Stand*.

1998   Appears in *Murder at 1600*, *Down in the Delta*, *U.S. Marshals*, and *Blade*; receives honorary doctorate degree in humanities and fine arts from SUNY; added to Hollywood Walk of Fame on August 21.

2000   Appears in *The Art of War*.

ANNOTATED FILMOGRAPHY

Art of War (2000): Snipes must stop a plot to destroy the United Nations building in this action/espionage thriller.

Blade (1998): Snipes is Blade, part human, part vampire out to get a monster plotting domination of the world; based on a character created for Marvel Comics.

U.S. Marshals (1998): Action thriller, with Snipes as Mark Sheridan, a C.I.A. operative on the run after a plane crash.

Down in the Delta (1998): As Will, Snipes is one of a cast of characters who aid a down-and-out single mother in the Mississippi Delta for the summer.

Murder at 1600 (1998): Washington homicide cop Harlan Regis (Snipes) is trying to find out who killed a White House staffer in an Oval Office bathroom.

One Night Stand (1997): Snipes plays Max Carlyle, a TV commercial director whose plastic world changes when he has an interracial affair.

The Fan (1996): Robert De Niro has an unhealthy passion for the San Francisco Giants and their $40 million star, Bobby Rayburn (Snipes).

To Wong Foo, Thanks for Everything! Julie Newmar (1995): Snipes is Noxeema Jackson, one of three drag queens heading for Hollywood when their car breaks down.

Waiting to Exhale (1995): Snipes took no credits in this story of four black women trying to find decent men in their lives.

Money Train (1995): Snipes costars with Woody Harrelson as two NYC transit cops involved in the theft of a subway car full of money.

Sugar Hill (1994): Snipes is Roemello Skuggs, a Harlem drug lord trying to get out.

Drop Zone (1994): As Pete Nessip, U.S. marshal, Snipes goes against some skydiving crooks.

Demolition Man (1993): It's the year 2032. A blond Snipes, as dangerous criminal Simon Phoenix, is pitted against Sylvester Stallone; both characters have been awakened after thirty-six years of deep-freeze.

Rising Sun (1993): Snipes is an L.A. cop working with wordly detective Sean Connery to investigate a homicide involving a U.S. senator and a Japanese corporation.

Boiling Point (1993): Federal agent Jimmy Mercer (Snipes) is out to find the man responsible for killing his friend and colleague.

Passenger 57 (1992): Antiterrorist expert John Cutter (Snipes) finds himself in the middle of an airline hijacking.

The Waterdance (1992): Story of a young novelist learning to readjust after a hiking accident leaves him paralyzed. Snipes plays Raymond Hill, one of the patients at the rehabilitation center.

White Men Can't Jump (1992): Snipes teams with Woody Harrelson; the two play basketball hustlers.

Jungle Fever (1991): An interracial affair, with Flipper Purify (Snipes) as a happily married man who crosses the line with his secretary.

New Jack City (1991): Ex-cops help to bring down Harlem drug lord Nino Brown (Snipes).

Mo' Better Blues (1990): A backstage look at a self-centered jazz pianist, with Snipes (playing Shadow Henderson, a jazz saxophonist) as his rival.

King of New York (1990): A band of black drug leaders take on their rivals, with Thomas Flanigan (Snipes), a tough cop, in pursuit.

Major League (1989): A baseball team owner tries to get out of her contract by organizing a team to lose games. Snipes is Willie Mays Hays, who can't hit the ball.

Vietnam War Story 2 (1989): Snipes is one of the soldiers greatly affected by the war in Vietnam.

Critical Condition (1987): Snipes is the ambulance driver in this Richard Pryor comedy about a con artist taking charge of a prison hospital.

Streets of Gold (1986): A former boxing champ trains two street kids for the U.S. boxing team. Snipes plays Roland Jenkins, a cocky young boxer.

Wildcats (1986): Goldie Hawn gets to coach a varsity team at a tough urban high school, with Snipes playing Trumaine, one of her players.

FURTHER READING

Buch, Gail. "I Won't Make the Same Mistake." *Parade*, August 8, 1993.

Farah, Caesar E. *Islam*. 4th ed. New York: Barrons, 1987.

Finch, Debra M., and Ruth S. Hunter. *Parents' Guide to Martial Arts*. Hartford, Conn.: Turtle Press, 1998.

Mitchell, David. *The Young Martial Arts Enthusiast*. New York: DK, 1997.

Rafkin, Louise. *The Tiger's Eye, The Bird's Fist: A Beginner's Guide to the Martial Arts*. Boston: Little, Brown, 1997.

Severson, Molly. *Performing Artists*, vol. 3. Detroit: Gale, 1995.

"A Snipes Attack." *New York Post*, February 21, 1994.

"Wesley Snipes On . . ." *Ebony*, November 1997.

"Wesley's Way." *New York Daily News*, November 13, 1997.

INDEX

INDEX

INDEX

PICTURE CREDITS

———— ❦ ————

ROSE BLUE, an author and educator, has written more than 50 books, both fiction and nonfiction, for young readers. Her books have appeared as TV specials and have won many awards. A native New Yorker, she lives in the borough of Brooklyn.

CORINNE NADEN, a former U.S. Navy journalist and children's book editor, also has more than 50 books to her credit. A freelance writer, she lives in Tarrytown, New York, where she shares living quarters with her two cats, Tigger and Tally Ho!